Hubert Comte
English translation: Jeremy Drake

Louvre Junior

English edition

NATHAN

By the same author

On Art

À la découverte de l'art (Hachette)
(Prix de la fondation de France)
L'aventure de l'art (Nathan)
La vie silencieuse. Natures mortes (Casterman)
Trésors d'Art en Europe (Ed. Epargne)
Écrits sur la peinture (Volets verts)

Essays

Des outils et des hommes (le Livre de Poche)
Le Paroir, la compagnie des outils (Desforges)
Le Tour de l'olivier (Régine Vallée)
Le Microscope (Casterman)
L'Huître (Volets verts)

Narratives

En France. La ville ancienne (Volets verts)
S'il faisait beau, nous passions par les quais (EFR)
La Force de la colère. Récits de Dachou (Stock)

Archeological crypt: the dungeon

A Dungeon, A Palace,
A Museum, A History Book

In 1180, when Philip II — later called Augustus — became king of France at the age of fifteen, Paris was at the mercy of a sudden attack by the Anglo-Normans. They held Gisors and the Vexin. Insecurity was rife: the enemy might have appeared by land or by water. In times of danger, great iron chains would be stretched across the river. In 1190 the King was getting ready to go on a Crusade. He left behind a will in which he ordered Parisians to surround their city with a continuous wall reinforced by turrets and fortified gates. Thus the city was to be equipped with two concentric ramparts: that of the inner *Cité* and the new surrounding wall. At the point on the right bank where the wall encountered the river, a mighty fortification was raised: the Louvre. The layout of the castle was simplicity itself: four straight walls formed a square with a tower in the middle of each wall and a tower at each corner. In the centre of the courtyard there was an impressive dungeon: 31 metres high, 19 metres in diamètre at its base. It was surrounded by a deep moat, so that even if the enemy managed to reach its foot, they would still not hold the heart of the fortress.

The treasury and the arsenal

"The Louvre castle",
miniature from *The Duke of Berry's Book of Hours*, 15th century

On the Limbourg brothers' miniature that decorates *The Duke of Berry's Book of Hours* for the month of October, one can easily recognize the simple layout of the castle and its dungeon. In front lies the bright new wall with its battlements and towers. In the foreground, one peasant is sowing while another one works the harrow. Behind them one can see a scarecrow in the shape of a hunter armed with a bow.

The dungeon became the symbol of the feudal and military power of the King of France. It housed the royal treasury and the archives — invaluable for proving claims to land. Some distinguished prisoners were held there, and in the early thirteenth century it became an arsenal.

Philip Augustus did not reside at the Louvre as he found it too uncomfortable, but under Saint Louis and Philip the Fair the castle was redecorated, and meetings and festivities were held there.

A love of illuminated books

Paris was growing constantly, and by the time Charles V was crowned in 1364, the Louvre could no longer act as an advance bastion: it became the king's palace instead. Its private apartments and reception rooms set a framework for the sovereign's well-ordered life.

Yet, as in a fairy tale, no one had noticed the establishment in the king's retinue of a prince from another stock. He would triumph over stupidity, survive conflagrations and escape cataclysms, before finally, six centuries later, possessing the entire palace. He would be the sovereign, destined to a long and brilliant future. His name: Art. The seed was sown in 1367 on the day Charles V had his library transferred to the Louvre: several hundred illustrated volumes of valuable and beautiful miniatures.

"Our castel of the Louvre"

Kings deserted the austere residence until 1528, when Francis I made this announcement: "Inasmuch as our intention is from now on to spend the greater part of our residence and habitation in our good town and city of Paris and its environs, more than in any other place in the kingdom, and recognizing that our castel of the Louvre is a more convenient and suitable environment for our accommodation, to this end we have resolved to have the said castel repaired and put in good order." Pierre Lescot was the architect of a façade that came to be admired as one of the purest masterpieces of the French renaissance. Jean Goujon decorated

The colonnade of Claude Perrault

it with bas-reliefs of remarkable vigour and sensitivity. It housed great rooms, spectacular staircases, and the luxurious ceiling of the king's bedroom. Catherine de' Medici, Queen Mother and Regent, had a palace prepared in the Tuileries gardens. Plans were drawn up to link it to the Louvre. This project was completed by Henry IV. Early in his reign, Louis XIV lived in the Louvre with part of his collections. The colonnade shown here dates from this time. Later, towards 1682, the king installed the seat of his monarchy at Versailles but authorized academicians and artists to use the Louvre's premises. Art had returned to the palace.

A museum and its light

In the Cour Carrée (Square Court), Pierre Lescot wing

During the reign of Louis XVI the idea of using the royal collections as the basis of a museum was launched. In 1793 the Convention decreed the opening of a museum. Property seized by the revolutionaries was added to the collections. Hubert Robert's plan for the redesigning of the Grand Gallery was enthusiastically received. Under Napoleon I the museum had an intelligent and zealous director: Vivant Denon. Building work was undertaken, additions were demolished, works of art which were supposed to be returned to their owners were installed. No matter, the momentum had been given.

An invisible force was constantly at work. The museum was expanding, the need for proper presentation of works had been understood, and their lighting had become an issue. However, the Louvre was still a palace when the Tuileries burned down in 1871. Rapid reconstruction

Project for the redesigning of the Great Hall of the Louvre, Hubert Robert (1733-1808)

established once and for all the design of this flagship monument.

One day in 1989 the Minister of Finance left his office in the rue de Rivoli for good. The pyramid, a sign of the Grand Louvre, was now in place. It reflects the ordered architecture of the past, and is also a sign of our times. Its elemental simplicity warms the heart and entices the sunlight down to the subterranean hallway — the place where, with beating heart, you let your enthusiasms guide you. The light moulds the forms of the sculptures, shimmers in the colours of the paintings, that brightness without which our artists — our guiding lights — could not have produced their masterpieces.

Senynefer and Hatshepsut (painted limestone) c.1410 B.C.

Egyptian Antiquities

1826: The year when this department was founded is not so very distant from us, especially when you consider the extremely long history of the Land of the Nile. And yet, just think of the fundamental changes in circumstances and mentalities! Then, consuls of Britain and France were organizing digs and accumulating amazing collections with a view to selling the objects. Charles X of France, urged on by Champollion — the decipherer of hieroglyphics, decided to acquire the whole lot. The objects were displayed in new, specially arranged rooms, decorated with paintings inspired by the Age of the Pharaohs. Egyptology became a speciality of French archeologists, and some of the objects discovered by Auguste Mariette came to enlarge the collections. The most recent acquisition is the huge head of Amenophis IV. It was given by the Egyptian government in recognition of France's assistance during the transfer of the temple of Abu Simbel to save it from the rising waters behind the Aswan Dam.

A key position

The seated scribe (painted limestone) c.2620-2350 B.C.

Among the ancient texts found in Egypt, one speaks directly to our hearts. It is a letter from a father urging his son to become a scribe. He describes the advantages of the profession: it is sedentary, clean, not very tiring, and it enables one to get close to the great of this world. Without the scribe it is impossible to write, take notes, make inventories or even prepare those famous books so necessary for the dead when they travel to the beyond. This scribe makes one think of a secretary, reed in hand, waiting for words to be dictated. In fact, as we know from other examples, some important man in high political office chose this position for his funerary statue.

The representation of a lifelike body, the illusion of life given by the glass eyes and the size of the statue have rightly made it the object of a "pilgrimage" for a great many visitors to the Louvre.

What the blue animal says

The peaceful "river horse", completely herbivorous, could only be dangerous to man on account of its considerable weight, and even then, only if it felt that it or its offspring were threatened. Hunting the hippopotamus was a favourite sport of the noble and powerful men of Ancient Egypt. Often, on the walls of tombs, the deceased is represented as drawing a bow or throwing a javelin to kill this aquatic pachyderm. The act had a symbolic value: the noble did not hesitate to risk his life in order to save his people from the horrible monsters that lurked in the marshlands.

The clumsy silhouette of the hippopotamus is modeled with an acute sense of essentials. The ceramic is covered with blue glaze, reflecting the colour of water, the animal's natural habitat. The plants drawn in black on its surface help us to imagine it swimming through them at the bottom of the river.

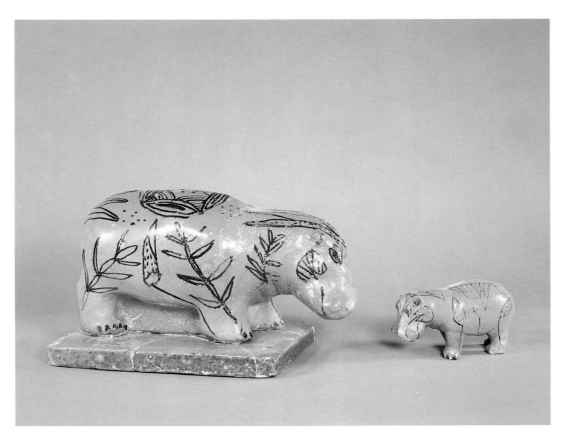

Hippopotamuses (pottery) c.2000 B.C.

On the river of the Great Beyond

Model of a boat (painted wood) c.1960 B.C. (Tomb of Nakhti at Assyut)

This boat — measuring 80 cm. in length — was found in the tomb of Nakhti, a Chancellor from the twelfth dynasty (1991-1928 B.C.). At the prow, the master of the ship keeps an eye on the horizon, takes soundings of the river bottom with the aid of a pole and commands the crew. Behind him, eight rowers facing backwards are each holding one oar. Above them rises the mast and its yards to which the sail will be fixed to catch the slightest breeze. The man at the tiller, the helmsman, guides the boat with the aid of two large oars. In the stern one can see the same elegant design as on papyruses or bas-reliefs. This boat replaced or represented the one the chancellor would need for travelling on the river of the Great Beyond, in particular for going to worship Osiris, the god of the dead, at Abydos.

Forever alive

Though their bodies are partly or wholly missing, Senynefer and Hatshepsut seem to hold their heads up all the more boldly. This man and woman, holding each other tight, impose their presence by the alertness of their wide open eyes staring out at the world, by their smiling mouths that seem to be on the point of saying something, and by the tension in their slightly straining necks, which seems to mean, "Here I am". The man's skin tone is reddish ochre, and the woman's complexion saffron — as tradition dictated — and they are joyfully contemplating the inhabitants of the land of eternity.

The back of their chair is a stela, inscribed with a prayer. Thanks to it, Senynefer and Hatshepsut will be nourished for centuries to come. The sculptor's logic is impeccable: the doubles of eternal beings must themselves radiate with life. The artist portrays the vital spark itself.

The ceremonial journey

The Book of the Dead from Nebquad, detail (papyrus), c.1400 B.C.

Papyrus scrolls were widely available in Ancient Egypt, enabling the preservation and diffusion of knowledge, the exchange of letters and the creation of literary works. Thanks to them we have a detailed knowledge of the lives of the pharaohs' subjects. The stalk of the plant is cut into thin strips that are then laid out in crossed rows, moistened, pressed and dried in order to produce a narrow scroll that can be several yards in length. Armed with his reed, the scribe or artist could set to work. The *Book of the Dead* was a guide to accompany the deceased in the Great Beyond. From left to right in the illustration one can successively see a procession of relatives, wailing women, Anubis and the box containing the canopic jars on a sledge pulled by several men, the deceased's mummy lying on a funeral barque drawn by oxen, some rows of offerings and, finally, the ritual scene of the opening of the deceased's mouth at his awakening.

What an awe-inspiring journey! Everyone would have thought about it with mixed feelings of confidence and foreboding.

Under the sign of the solar disk

Under the name of Aten (disk), the sun became the object of an exclusive cult for Pharaoh Amenophis IV (c.1365-1349 B.C.), who took the name of Akhenaten (favoured of Aten). This caused great disruption from the top to the bottom of society, for the priests and followers of the former religion suddenly found themselves cult-less and powerless. Curiously, this revolution had a very profound effect on the arts: the pharaoh imposed his silhouette and his face as canons of beauty. However, he was clearly marked by disease or degeneracy: his face was unnaturally long, he had a protruding chin, his slender limbs emphasized the heaviness of his hips and the thickness of his thighs. All members of the royal family were represented in this way, in scenes whose informal charm is often most touching. However, few vestiges remain of the art of Amarna, the new capital, as Akhenaten's successor reestablished the former cult and destroyed or disfigured the images of what was from then on considered a heresy.

Amenophis IV (limestone), 1365-1349 B.C. (Karnak)

The good goddess's welcome

Hathor, goddess of joy and love, also presided over dance and guided navigators, in particular those on funerary barques. She is portrayed in different ways: a sycamore nursing a child, a cow wearing a great necklace, a woman with horns that enclose the red disk of the Sun.

Wearing a tight dress and a layered wig, she welcomes King Seti I on his departure from the land of the living, making him touch her necklace, the symbol of her being. The pharaoh wears a pearl pectoral and, over an apron loincloth, a long, pleated, transparent dress. The scene is solemn and fraternal: there is the intensity of the looks they exchange, the parallelism of the gestures that evoke a dance, the vigorous clasping of hands. The pharaoh moves forward as an equal of a god. His eternal life is now a certainty.

The goddess Hathor and King Seti I (painted limestone), c.1303-1290 B.C. Height: 2.26 m.

Egyptian design

Chair (wood), c. 1350 B.C.

This chair is more than 3000 years old, and yet nothing separates us from it. We are familiar with the string bottoming, the curves of the seat's back which accomodate our own. We can appreciate the gold and various-wood marquetry, and the blue paint on the four short legs is of the utmost good taste. The solid construction on four lion's paws is wholly satisfactory. It is an item of furniture we should willingly have in our home. The explanation for this could well be that the Egyptian artist who designed this chair was totally immersed in the artistic culture of his time and his place, without much individual imagination or desire for novelty. He was looking, rather, for shapes that would blend into each other, basic hues that would harmonize, contours as simple as possible. Such stylization, such refinement go beyond fashion and can speak to people of another time and another place in a language they can understand.

The king crawling on his knees

This little stone statuette always attracts the visitor's eye. Indeed, among so many representations of human beings, it is one of the very few sculptures to show the effort of a man in action. The man is none other than the pharaoh himself, as we can tell from his head-dress, an emblem of his dignity. His position is one the monarch adopted every year at the start of the Nile flood: crawling in the temple courtyard, pushing an offering towards the statue of the god. The sculpture is a document of artistic technique, for it is an original scale model, cut by an artist. Handed over to a skilful professional, it could be copied or enlarged. Several details are proof of this: the traces of rough hewing (systematic and broadly outlined) on the head and shoulders, and an indi-

The crawling pharaoh

cation in black ink of the pleats on the loin-cloth.

Some objects produced in great quantities give an impression of uniformity. Here we are present at a birth, in the studio of a great artist.

Eternal rest

The Greek historian Herodotus has given us a first-hand account of the embalming techniques of the Ancient Egyptians. The dead body was cut open in order to remove the organs that were susceptible to decomposition. These were then placed in special jars. The body was soaked in aromatic substances and immersed for seventy days in natron, a natural salt, which dessicated it. It was then wrapped in gauze bandages amongst which amulets would be placed. The mummy was laid in a sarcophagus and a copy of the *Book of the Dead* placed in the tomb.

The Egyptians believed in life in the hereafter and in the immortality of the soul. Death separated the soul from the body, but embalming enabled the soul to live in the body and animate it once more. The technique produced prodigious results: in the Cairo Museum the face of the great Ramses II projects impressive charisma and ardent authority. Looking at this mummy of a man causes one to reflect on this people's faith in the immortality of each individual, and also on the respect due to the remains of a man exposed to the public gaze. No one was meant to see them, to touch them or to move them. It is only right that we grant them a moment's silence.

Mummy of a man, 3rd or 2nd century B.C.

The Victory of Samothrace (The Winged Victory) (marble)
c.190 B.C. (Greece). Height: 3.28 m.

Greek, Etruscan and Roman Antiquities

These were the first masterpieces to find their place in the Louvre — and who would wonder at that? Scholars in the time of Francis I read the original texts of Greek and Latin authors. The king collected Mediterranean antiquities. Richelieu and Mazarin followed in his footsteps, while the First and Second Empires saw the addition of the important Borghese and Campana collections.

The first face

If one goes back through the course of Greek art history, just before disappearing into the mists of time, one stumbles upon the idols of the Cyclades. The typical idol has a simplified human body, the nose projecting from a smoothly curved face, the crossed arms marked by a slight incision on the chest. Another incision indicates two separate legs. There are no clues as to the interpretation and no inscriptions. Imagination must take over: one might conjure up a female divinity worshipped by a people under her care, providing abundance here on earth and happiness in the hereafter. The goddess's morphology indicates the idea that her worshippers had of her. A human without eyes or a mouth, dispensing with gestures. She is above men: she knows without seeing, commands without speaking, intervenes without hands and moves without walking. She is pure magic, pure power, pure breath of life.

Female head (marble), c.2500 B.C.
(Cyclades). Height: 27 cm.

A master draughtsman

Crater of Euphronios, c.510 B.C. (Attica)

The Greek word *crater* refers to a large wide-necked vase with two handles. The Ancients used it for holding a mixture of water and wine. This one bears a famous signature: the vase painter Euphronios's. The scene depicted is Hercules fighting the giant Antæus. Three female spectators are horrified but fascinated by the violence of the blows the two protagonists exchange. Like spectators the world over, they anxiously await the outcome. The hero is holding the giant in a for-

midable grip, his face convulsed with pain. Notice the perfection of the outlines and the genius of the composition: the wrestler on the left, seen in profile, is coiled up, ready to pounce. The torso on the right, seen full face, looks like a fallen statue. This is a terrible moment: the entangled bodies are immobilised, the vice of the arms is tightening, the pain is increasing. Soon we shall hear the cracking of bones, of vertebræ... Even at this early date the prodigious labours of Hercules were being depicted.

The banquet of life

Sarcophagus of a married couple (terracotta), late 6th century B.C. (Estruscan art). Length: 1.90 m.

Terracotta sculptures of this size are rare as they are a technical tour de force. They cannot be solid, for the damp centre would make them burst during baking. The artist has to model statues that are hollow and thin, but this makes them fragile and awkward to handle. Before it dries, clay can lose its shape. The solution has often been to construct a sculpture in several parts and to hide the joins, in the folds of a garment for example. The mar-

ried couple on this Etruscan sarcophagus are portrayed as guests reclining at table, the bust raised and elbows resting on cushions. The man's hand is placed tenderly on his wife's shoulder. Their eyes are wide open, their lips slightly upturned, their faces smiling. Egyptian sarcophaguses always seem like conveyances for the hereafter. The Etruscans, by contrast, chose to make a happy moment in life last for ever.

"Stay on our ship, O Victory"

The Greek historian Thucydides wrote, "The navy is not an occasional activity. It must be a full-time effort". In Greece, the maritime states fought at sea for their independence, or to defend their way of life and ideals of freedom against a foreign invader. However, at sea the outcome of a battle is far from certain: adverse winds and waves can destroy a fleet. What can be done? Keep the goddess on your side by erecting a magnificent statue in her honour! So a winged woman is elegantly poised at the prow of a stone ship. One can almost hear her clothing slapping in the wind while the spray makes the wet fabric stick to her chest, stomach and thighs, the "prow" of her own body, facing the air of the open sea.

See photo p. 20.

A roman impressionist

Funeral procession (Roman painting), late 1st century B.C.

Fresco painting is a special technique. The artist brushes the colours onto a still-damp limestone surface that, once dry, cannot be repainted. Since the coating forms part of the wall itself, one can understand how, in a dry and mild climate, a fresco can last for hundreds of years, like the buildings it decorates. In Rome this painting from the late first century B.C. embellished the tomb of a doctor of Greek origin called Patron. Thanks to the inscriptions above the heads of the figures, it has been possible to identify the deceased's wife and two daughters. Accompanied by her grand-children the widow is probably on her way to meditate at the tomb. The atmosphere is unreal: the diaphanous figures float like shadows between the trees that are no bigger than they are. The message of this elegant and wistful funeral procession could well be that the illusions of life come face to face with those of the hereafter. Visiting the dead has its purpose: it is a first lesson in separation.

"Bread and circuses"

Roman crowds would shout their famous cry, *panem et circenses* to demand "bread and circuses" from their rulers. The circus games were highly varied: wild-animal fights, lion and tiger hunts, gladiator combats, wrestling, boxing, and also miniature naval battles. Clearly, promoters had fertile imaginations even then! This man is a champion of *pancratium*, a cross between wrestling and boxing. He has just kept his opponent at a distance with a kick to the tibia. If his opponent loses his balance and falls forwards, two fearsome fists will spring into action. This is a down-to-earth, crowd-pleasing work, displaying a remarkable sense of observation. Such statuettes were produced in single copies following the "lost wax" process. The object was modeled in wax and then covered with potter's clay. When fired, the mould let the hot wax drain off, and molten bronze could flow into the empty space. The mould was then broken in order to free the statue.

Wrestler (Roman bronze found at Autun), 1st century A.D.
Height: 27 cm.

A pictorial welcome

Servants at a banquet (detail of a Roman mosaic at Carthage), c.A.D. 180.

I magine how the archeologists removing the soil covering the floor of an old Roman house must have felt when they suddenly caught sight of this carpet of small chunks of marble and glass paste. Mosaics are particularly suitable for decorating the floors of Mediterranean houses. Light brings out the colours splendidly, and when the floor is damp, it gives off a delightful illusion of coolness. In addition, upkeep is extremely simple. The subjects chosen have the charm of great variety: mythological scenes as in the house in Antioch, the imitation of a carpet for one in Daphne, or even a depiction of work and play in everyday life.

Here we have a slice of reality: the procession of servants bringing food and ustensils for a feast The image is realistic, the gestures true to life. The host's message is clear: "You will be well received here and will lack nothing".

Of sand and fire

How many caring hands, how many years of protective burial were needed to preserve this goblet up to our times? Due to its fragility we view this simple object with as much respect as for recognized masterpieces. It too bears witness in its way. It tells of the virtuosity of ancient Syrian glassmakers, long famous throughout the Mediterranean. One can imagine the captivating dance of the glass blower turning the still soft, red-hot ball at the end of the metal rod into which he is blowing. Embellished with ribbons of glass, the goblet has become a mysterious flower bearing the imprint of the artist-craftsman and his lively imagination. This glass, designed to hold water, seems to have retained something of its earlier liquid state.

Goblet, 4th century A.D. (Syria, Roman civilization)

The Archers of Darius (enamelled brick), c.500 B.C. (Susa)

Oriental Antiquities

In 1881 the Louvre had to house the finds of French diplomats stationed in Iraq. These included the remains of Nineveh, of Sargon's palace at Khorsabad, and of the Sumerian civilization at Tello. The new department functioned as an active institution, linked to archeological research, and many of the curators shared their time between digs in Iraq and the presentation of collections in Paris. By a natural process, this department also acquired Islamic objects from the same region. One is often carried away by the beauty of exhibits in the Louvre, but here one is gripped by the magic they convey.

Gudea (diorite), c.2150 B.C. (South Mesopotamia)

A statue at prayer

In the days when the Louvre was a palace housing a private gallery, artists would come to paint and draw. Copying masterpieces of the past was, quite rightly, part of the apprenticeship of art. It is moving to think of the anonymous copyists who earned a living from this trade and who helped to broaden the audience for art at a time when art reproductions did not exist. Great artists also set themselves to this meticulous and humble task: Delacroix, Van Gogh, Cézanne, Renoir, Matisse, Giacometti. A young contemporary painter of Argentine origin, Ricardo Cavallo, has made this drawing of the statue of Gudea, a Sumerian governor of Lagash. The dignitary is both serious and meditative. The statue, portraying him in eternal prayer, was intended to replace him in the god's temple.

Gudea, drawing by Ricardo Cavallo

The king's judgment

A basalt stela taller than a man was found in Susa in 1901-02 by Jacques de Morgan and the members of his mission. It had been set up to honour Hammurabi, the sixth king of the Babylonian dynasty. This inscribed stone, dating from the first half of the 18th century B.C., had been set up in a city in Babylonia before being taken to Susa as a prize of war by the Elamites in the twelfth century B.C. At its summit, face to face, are the king and the sun-god Shamash. On the body of the pillar there is, not a code of law exactly, but a collection of the most significant royal judgments.

Hammurabi's code of law (basalt), 18th century B.C. (Susa).
Height: 2.25 m.

A right royal dress

Between the third and the second millenia B.C., the Elamite civilization crossed the frontier with Iran to reach Bactria in central Asia, currently northern Afghanistan. There, important personalities were accompanied in their tombs by everyday objects that had belonged to them and also by luxurious items, veritable works of art that reflected their social status. Were they intended to be useful to the deceased in the here- after or were they offerings specially prepared for burial — who can say? The face is in limestone, the hands probably were also. The dress is in grey stone, and its design — crinoline with swaying woollen fringes — is modelled on the clothes of the Elamite queens. The overall line is vigorous, and the desire to communicate majesty by the ample proportions is perfectly realized. This statue gives a joyous impression of good health and freshness with just a hint of humour.

Statuette of a woman,
early 2nd millenium B.C. (Bactria)

The entrance to Sargon's palace

The Assyrian king Sargon II, whose reign marks the highpoint of his country's power, built himself a palace within the citadel of a newly founded city near Nineveh: Khorsabad.
Before the gates of the royal residence, winged bulls with human heads kept guard. These mythical creatures dated back to the ancient Sumerians (c.2000 B.C.) for whom, as emblems of the sun, they personified the mountains of the east, from behind which the sun rose. Combining the strength of a bull, the wisdom of a mature man and the speed of a bird, these truly invincible beings kept watch over the foundations of the world, guaranteeing the palace's eternity. The artist gives detail to the animal's body: prominent ribs, thigh muscles, veins on the legs. Yet he also adopts stylization: the fur is portrayed by decorative curls that are continued in the hair and the beard. Wall and wing are connected in a most gra-

cious manner. The fifth leg enables one to have both a side, walking view and a frontal, stationary view. Between the legs an inscription proclaims: "The palace of Sargon, the great King, the mighty king, King of the Universe, King of Assyria".

Assyrian winged bull (gypsum), 721-705 B.C. (Palace of Sargon II). Height: 4.20 m.

The famous "Immortals"

S hod in light sandals, clothed in trousers tied tight around the ankles and their official dress, the archers of Darius' personal guard hold their spears with both hands, their bows and quivers hung on their backs. Their beards and hair are arranged with regulation care. They stare straight ahead like birds of prey, and the whites of their eyes are set like windows in the dark colour of their skin. The sculptors at Susa, around 500 B.C., modelled and enamelled the bricks before aligning them to form a wall. The intervening gaps parallel the vertical lines of the spears and the clothing, while the horizontals suggest an unending change of station. These soldiers defended the palace, by their image alone, in the event that the flesh-and-blood guards happened to be absent.

See photo p. 28

The noble art of falconry

E ven today, Saudi Arabian princes pay daily visits to their falcons and to their trainers and guardians. This fierce bird of prey nose-dives onto birds and rolls on the ground with them. It can immobilize a rabbit with its unerring claw before despatching it with a blow from its hooked beak. It will then wait for its master, for the hunting bird knows the falconer will reward it. It then takes up its position on the gloved fist, the eyes covered by a hood. This is what an Iranian artist of the Seljuk period has depicted in the marvellously untrammelled design decorating this bowl. The potters possessed techniques of painting and firing that are still unknown to Europeans. Not only could they achieve extreme refinement of design, but they also used a great number of colours including gold, and they knew how to produce a splendid shimmering effect.

Bowl, late 12th-early 13th century A.D. (Iran)

Her Feast Day (brush and wash tint), Goya, 1796

Graphic Arts

This is a much more important domain than might at first seem to be the case. "Art on paper" can be produced with pencil, pen, watercolour, wash tint or pastel, but also includes engravings and illustrated books. The department was started when Louis XIV acquired the collection of Jabach, a Cologne banker, in 1671. Later, the studio archives of the "principal painters" of the king constituted a nucleus enriched with emigrés' property seized by the revolutionaries. Finally there have been generous donations from the Rothschilds, David-Weills and others. The masterpieces of this department, which are fragile and extremely sensitive to the action of light, are made public in temporary exhibitions.

Tender and mischievous

Young girl, Rubens, 1577-1640

Rubens, the painter of the life of Marie de' Medici (in the Louvre) was a multi-talented man. To start with, there was his artistic genius — evident as much in his imagination as in his technique; then there was his great intelligence, which brought him ambassadorial postings; he had material comfort, the serene joys of family life, and lastly there was his natural tendency to find happiness in all things.

It bursts into evidence in this bold drawing in which the painter conveys his joy in capturing the first feminine wiles of a very young girl. One can easily imagine the scene as she tries out her powers. She smiles in order to charm, but, out of the corner of her eye, takes note of the reaction. Rubens goes beyond merely clever resemblance to tell us a story. He needs no words.

Fun that went wrong

Goya undertook an exemplary journey into his own innermost depths, and an astonishing trip it was. At first he was very much in vogue as a designer of tapestries, soon after, as a portraitist of kings and nobles. He also showed virtuosity in portraying street life. Nothing escaped him: a facial type, an attitude, the soft glow of velvet or the brilliance of satin. He was genuinely close to the people, and did not live in an ivory tower. Like a reporter, he bore witness in his drawings and paintings to the horrors of the war between France and the Spanish people. Another event cruelly marked him: his deafness, which cut him off from others. So he cut himself off even further — and painted his worst nightmares on the walls of his house. His last views were of bullfighting. A ferocious image of malice, *Her Feast Day* presents two people, one of whom is a degenerate, pretending to be having fun with a third person, whom they are, in fact, terrorising and torturing.

Reproduction p. 34.

Grasp the moment, the fleeting colours

Sketchbook, Morocco, Delacroix, 1830.

Delacroix filled seven sketchbooks in the course of a journey through Morocco from late January to late April 1832. Watercolours, drawings, landscapes, portraits, details of clothing, of jewelry, of horses' harnesses are mixed in with jottings in which one can sense paintings in gestation. Thus on 11 April he wrote; "Aïn El Dahliah. Mounted Caddour's horse as mine was ill. Had another look at some beautiful olive trees on a hillside. Noticed the shadows cast by stirrups and feet. Shadow always forms the outline of the thigh and the leg below. The stirrup sticks out, but the straps are unseen. The stirrup and the breast buckle very white, mat... Grey horse, bridled, worn white velvet. Ink in the people in brown, highlighting them if necessary so they stand out."

The Lacemaker, Vermeer, 1635-1675. 24 × 21 cm.

Paintings

A single figure can give an idea of the size of the collection: more than 6000 paintings from the principal countries of Europe, from the twelfth to the middle of the nineteenth centuries. Some paintings had been acquired by Francis I; Louis XIV systematically built up the collection according to his own tastes. In 1750, long before the Convention's famous decree of 1793, the project was established of a museum where all French people could see the paintings in the royal collections. Until then they had decorated the walls of royal residences or slumbered in depots. Under Louis XVI, Count d'Angiviller, Director of Monuments, prepared the Grand Gallery of the Louvre for the displaying of paintings and made numerous acquisitions in order to complete the collection. The idea was established. The founding of the museum, the revolutionary seizures of emigré property, the Napoleonic project, the efforts of curators and the generosity of donors all contributed to the further building up of the collection.

A dizzy gaze towards the infinite

The Virgin with Chancellor Rolin,
Jan Van Eyck, c.1435

A man is praying on his knees, his hands joined above a book of hours. He is solemn and dressed in a fur-lined coat. The room opens directly onto the outside, onto a very real world. The apparition, on the other hand, is super-natural: an angel rises up with beating wings, ready to place a golden crown on the head of Mary. The young woman's eyes are cast down; she is the servant of the Lord. She holds her child away from her as he, carry-ing in his left hand a globe surmounted with a cross, blesses the donor with his right. Notice the beauty of the portraits, the majestic fall of the folds on Mary's robe. In the distance, life carries on for symbolic lilies, birds and people out for a stroll. As if Van Dyck had used a telescope, he shows tiny horsemen on a quayside, people crossing a bridge, travellers on a ferry, towers, belfries, fields, mountains. Creation, out to in-finity.

War on a black horse

In 1432 at San Romano, the Florentines defeated the army of Sienna. Como de' Medici, Duke of Florence, decided to keep a memento of this battle. Three paintings of three metres in length were commissioned from Paolo Uccello. Placed in the great hall of the palace they amazed visitors by their colours, the illusion of life they gave, and the science of the painter, who was a master of perspective.

Moreover, the arms and armour, decorated with gold and silver foil, shone like so many mirrors, giving the illusion of movement by reflecting the comings and goings of visitors. The painting can be read like a scene in a film: in the centre, Micheletto di Cotignola is shouting, "Attack!", while to the left the charge has started with lowered spears, and to the right and centre the cavalry is getting under way.

The Battle of San Romano, Paolo Uccello, c.1455

Evening on Golgotha

"Staging," the term might seem to belong to the world of theatre, and yet, this way of organizing an illusion of reality for spectators plays an essential role in painting. Objects have their place. Figures have not merely a position in space in relation to one another but also gestures and movements decided by the artist. In this Pietà of the Provençal school, everything is centred on the body of

Christ, which dominates the scene. The two men and two women are wrapt in thought or in suffering, each in their own way. The faces are vigorously sculpted by the light, the hands are admirably delicate and the draperies of wonderful nobility. The clear tones of the body and the clothing vie with the ground and the dark cloak, while in the distance the silhouette of Jerusalem stands out against the golden sky.

Pietà of Villeneuve lès Avignon, Enguerrand Quarton, c.1455

Contest for a crazy crew

The Ship of Fools, Hieronymus Bosch, c.1485-1500

The highly extravagant Hieronymus Bosch was brilliantly talented. With what delicacy he depicts the foliage, with what cruelty he represents the gestures and faces, how meticulously he sees the details! This is a strange boat indeed, one that nobody is steering and aboard which the passengers care only for having fun — for singing, drinking and eating. The monks and nuns, who should be setting an example, are hardly better than the average fool. Everything here is bizarre, hysterical, incongruous. The boat's mast is a tree at the top of which an owl is keeping watch. By climbing up the mast one can have one's share of the chicken. There are no sails attached to any of the ropes, though a loaf of bread is dangling from one of them. At the end of a pole an upturned jug serves as an emblem for these travellers who have a goodly stock of bottles, jugs and barrels. Emerging from the black water, a swimmer holds up a bowl, while another pushes the boat. To the right a kitchen implement is being used as a rudder. So what! Like some human follies, this escapade is going absolutely nowhere.

The near and the far

Away with banalities, with undreamt of wealth and romantic tales! Look at the painting itself if you have the opportunity, or else a reproduction — have a really good look. Measure the perfectly proportioned face: it is a strong face, with both male and female features. Feel its calm, withdrawn aspect, symbolising everyone's secret being. Let yourself be caught up in the illusion of the folds of the sleeve emerging from the shadows, and follow it along to the hands, so gentle, inscribed in an oval. Leave the balcony and flit about above the landscape in the background. It is rugged and mineral, reduced to essentials as in Chinese paintings of the Song period. Near each shoulder, notice the tracks of men trying to connect: the winding road in the hills and the arches of the bridge over the river. Notice also that the painter's brush has hidden all trace of itself. Take this vision away with you in your heart. Tell yourself to find words next time to describe the tones and colours. Come back.

Mona Lisa (La Joconde) Leonardo da Vinci, 1503-1507

The front and back of life

Carondelet Diptyche, Jean Gossaert, known as Mabuse, 1517

Four paintings grace the front and back of two hinged panels. Jean Carondelet, dean of the church of Besançon, advisor to Charles V and a friend of Erasmus, commissioned a portable religious painting from Jean Gossaert. This is first and foremost a portrait of Carondelet, allying forceful brushwork to delicate shaping of the face. The hands are joined in the traditional posture of a donor praying to the Virgin with Child. If you look on the other side, you will see two niches like those in chapels. The coat of arms indicates noble lineage, a sign of human inequality. In the second niche a masterly portrayal of a skull evokes the state of the body after death. The skull is facing upwards as though about to cry out, yet no sound can come out of this petrified mouth. The jaw has fallen off. Without life, without a soul, the body is a mere wreck. Earthly existence comes to an end; faith is the condition of eternal life.

"This is what I saw"

The Beggars, Breughel the Elder, 1568

Breughel was a complete artist, with a sense of observation and of imagination, a refined colorist and an impeccable draughtsman. In a strangely empty place, where a passerby walks on without noticing them, five beggars, three of whom are lepers with stumps instead of feet, are going their separate ways in search of a few coins.

Perhaps they will meet up again to pool their alms. One of them is wearing bells on his legs, and fox tails are clearly visible on the light coloured clothing of four of them: lepers had to indicate their presence so people could avoid them. Crutches and roughly carved artifical limbs add to the tragic, chaotic feel of the scene. Should one look for social or political significance (the headgear imitating that of the rich, the tails being emblems of the struggle against the Spanish)?

Breughel is showing that one day he saw leprosy. He also discovered that, when shared, the depths of misery are less hard to bear. Even the most miserable hang on to life.

Hands, cards and glances

The Cheats, Georges de la Tour, 1593-1652

Georges de la Tour is telling a story that happened in a tavern. A game of cards is being played for money. To the right, a chubby young man, rich, his clothes embroidered with gold, wearing a feather in his cap, has his mind on his play. To his right, the lady in pearls (she has them around her neck, on her ears and wrists and even in her hair) is hiding her cards and making a sign, while her servant offers her a glass of wine. On the table lie gold coins. The servant is having a good look at the other players' cards. Her service is a ruse, part of a plot to despoil the naive young man perhaps? The attractive figure to the left is asking for our attention, showing us his cards. His handsome, beribboned apparel hides a gesture that only we can see: his left hand is drawing an extra ace of diamonds from his belt.

What captivating colours and richness of cloth, what a zig-zagging of glances and a ballet of hands to show that appearances can be deceptive! This is both a painting and a fable.

Listening to the silence of things

Still life with wafers, Baugin, c.1630-1635

A still life is a painting that portrays inanimate objects, fruit for example, or food, household objects, musical instruments or books. The most striking thing about this painting by Baugin is the peacefulness and the distance between the objects, as thought they are three strangers who do not want to speak to each other. The background is in shadow, with a stone wall to the left. On a cloth-covered table we see a glass with a foot so fine that the wine seems to be hanging in mid-air, the liquid surface acting as a mirror. The bottle is covered in plaited straw. The pewter plate overhanging the edge of the table invites us to step into the painting. It reflects the light wafers that have been delicately rolled and set out in apparent disorder. In fact these seven tubes invite our eyes to follow them to see what is in the painting. These objects have been laid out by someone, a caring and affectionate wife. The traveller who will soon enter will see that he is welcome in this home.

The painter of heartfelt simplicity

The Pilgrims of Emmaus, Rembrandt, 1648

Luke the Evangelist tells us "And on that same day two of them went to a village called Emmaus. Whilst they were discussing all these events (the crucifixion), Jesus came up to them and went with them along the road. But their eyes were kept from recognizing him." They are drawing close to the village, Jesus pretends to carry on. "Stay with us", they say, "for it is getting late." When he took bread, blessed it, broke it

46

and gave it to them, their eyes were opened and they recognized him. At that moment he disappeared.

Deeply religious, and used to letting the light of the soul shine through the rags of paupers, Rembrandt recreates one moment: "They recognized him." The tavern servant enters. He feels that something that is beyond him has happened. This simple gesture echoes in the vastness. The three men are enthralled, the tablecloth glows with supernatural light. What is happening comes from on high.

A miraculous surprise

The Angels' Kitchen, Murillo, 1645-1648

The Superior has just opened the door of the refectory for a nobleman, hat in hand. The visitors stand stock still in bewilderment on the threshold. The cook, a monk, is in ecstasy. Celestial beings are busy doing his work. One angel is going to fetch some water while giving instructions to another; a third is laying the table, a fourth stirring the soup. Cherubs act as assiduous kitchen hands, preparing the vegetables, while the eldest crushes garlic with a pestle. In the corner a tilting cauldron, whose shape is a prolongation of the curves of the vault, sets its own brilliance off against the earthenware jug. Nothing is lacking: colourful vegetables, meat, a fire and a rustic pitcher on the table. The eye follows a deep curve and is lost in the shadows.

This painting by Murillo illustrates the reconciliation of prayer and action. Providence comes to the aid of the just. As Teresa of Avila said, "The Lord advances between the pots and pans."

The lacemaker

The painting is almost square. A diagonal, from top left to bottom right, cuts it in two. On the right-hand side the background is clear, with direct lighting on the loom, the dress and the face. Attenuated reflections of this lighting can be seen on the sleeve and the edge of the tablecloth. On the other side there is shadow: absolute at bottom left, dark under the table, with lighter shades on the hair, the dress and part of the hands. The fingers converge onto the invisible point which the eyes follow. Our eye strolls through this painting until stumbling, suddenly, upon an accident: red and white threads, colour and light in their purest form that spill over like two cascades — the violence of a trumpet call over a gentle flute-like painting.

Vermeer is telling us what painting is like, its apparent peacefulness inspired by the violence of the emotions. See photo page 38.

History written by a painter

The Coronation of Napoleon I, David, 1806-1807, 6.2 × 9.8 m.

Napoleon commissioned the painter David to "cover" the magnificent ceremony held on 2 December 1804. In the impressive setting of Notre-Dame Cathedral in Paris, Pope Pius VII is blessing Josephine. The sovereign himself is about to place the Empress's crown on his wife's head. The beauty of the women's and the prelates' dress, the uniforms of the marshalls and chamberlains, has from the start held the visitor's eye. Even more astonishing is the greatest portrait gallery there has ever been. David studied — sketches have survived — the face of each person in order to recreate the scene with authenticity.

News invades art

The Raft of the Méduse, Géricault, 1819, 4.91 × 7.16 m.

In 1818, at the age of 27, Géricault launched into an ambitious project: a painting of 35 square metres. The subject was to be the tragic adventure of the survivors of the *Méduse*, shipwrecked off the coast of Africa: twelve agonizing days and just fifteen survivors out of 149 passagers. The work was completed for the opening of the Salon; it had taken Géricault 16 months from his first sketches. He had read an account of the shipwreck, questioned survivors, and even constructed a model of the raft! He had studied people in the throes of death, corpses and mental patients and had found the time for a brief trip to Le Havre to see the sea. Over and above the representation of a real-life drama, official opinion saw in this painting the bewilderment of a rudderless generation. It was a failure for Géricault. Yet the work, which is also a portrait of the human condition, was displayed in towns all around England with great success. His destiny marked by a tragic star, Géricault died at the age of 32.

A painter fights with his weapons

In the space of three days, in late July 1830, the people of Paris rose up against Charles X. Inspired by what was happening, drawings seethed within the mind of Delacroix, the witness and visionary. The painting, exhibited at the 1831 Salon, was purchased by the new king.

Bare-breasted, brandishing the tricolor and holding a rifle, a woman wearing the revolutionaries' Phrygian bonnet is rushing forwards amid the dead bodies on the barricade: "Forwards!", she cries. Beyond the foreground of the wounded and dead, the army of the people is rising. To her left, a child with arms found in the street. In the distance: Notre Dame.

The bodies, the clothing, the faces, the weapons: everything is taken from life. So the aparition of this distinguished-looking, larger-than-life woman, Liberty, the mother of a people, is all the more impressive. The painting, considered an incitement to riot, was returned to the painter. Not until 1874 did it enter the Louvre.

Liberty Leading the People, Delacroix, 1830

Where does the earth end and the sky begin?

Landscape with a River and a Distant Bay, Turner, c.1845

Turner was magnificently unclassifiable. Was he a romantic, or a modern? Is this landscape a real place on earth, or rather a fancy of his imagination? One can approach this strange and beautiful painting by saying that whereas other painters paint the world as they see it, Turner painted the world as he remembered it. His subject was his wonderment, what remains when one has gone away, the taste rather than the appearance of the fruit. With his watercolours in hand, this adventurous artist sought out the most unusual effects of light, its violence, its tremulousness, its fusions. He would cling to a mast during a storm, or climb a mountain at night in order to catch the first rays of the sun on its summit.

Slave (marble), Michelangelo, 1513-1515. Height: 2.09 m.

Sculptures

A thousand works — French, for the most part — from romanesque art (11th century) right up to the great animal sculptor Barye (who died in 1875); monumental sculptures, such as those of Coustou, or more unobtrusive works such as Houdon's portraits, all invite the visitor to wander among them to discover the way light plays on their forms. Some countries of Europe are represented by very great names: the Germanic lands with Tilman Riemenschneider and above all Italy with the two "Slaves" by Michelangelo.

Stone shall speak!

In the course of history one can see that man has remained faithful to the dwelling places of his ancestors. Near Mont Beuvray (Bibractum, an important city of the Gauls), Autun (Augustodunum) was beautified after the Roman invasion with monumental edifices. During the twelfth century a cathedral was built in this town, its porch ornamented with an unforgettable "Last Judgment", devoted to Lazarus, the man whom Jesus resurrected. Brought back to life, swathed in his shroud, his limbs still in the linen wrappings, he was a source of fascination for Christians in the Middle Ages. What had he seen, this man who had conquered death? The faithful flocked in vast numbers to the pilgrimage church. For them a

Saint Peter, late 12th century (Autun)

group of statues was sculpted. Figures were "acting out" the scene. One of the spectators is Saint Peter, whose head we see here, a head most certainly sculpted by a great artist. His eyes are feasting on the amazing spectacle, his mouth is on the point of smiling, and, in a moment, the apostle will no longer be able to prevent himself from crying out his amazement at the sight of this prodigy, his joy in the victory and his faith in the one whose disciple he is.

The favourite disciple's distress

Saint John by the Cross (wood), late 15th century (Touraine)

Night has fallen. Jesus is there, lifeless, nailed to the cross between the two thieves. All is over, perhaps even hope is at an end. John, the beloved disciple, is still there waiting on one side, while Mary is on the other, tearless for having cried so much. What can be done at a time of such sorrow? Fall on the ground, like a child, and sob until the body's fountain is all dried up. This is what the sculptor of the crucifixion of Laché (in Touraine) has expressed perfectly. The apostle's eyes are cast down, the folds of his garments weep for him. The unknown artist who sculpted these folds, these hands, this tremulously youthful face, has his place among the greatest.

Veiled faces for a day of mourning

The Tomb of Philippe Pot (painted stone), late 15th century (Burgundy)

As one gazes on this group sculpture, in painted stone, one might well imagine hearing the tolling of a funeral bell. Philippe Pot, seneschal of the Duke of Burgundy before becoming chamberlain to the King of France, is being carried by eight mourners, clothed in black and carrying the coats of arms of their lord. They are bearing on their shoulders a mortuary slab representing the state bed upon which the deceased lies in his armour, his hands joined in prayer. At his feet lies his dog, a symbol of silent fidelity. In portraying a funeral procession the artist presents a vision of death different from eternal immobility; these eight faithful companions will endlessly conduct their master towards his destiny, to us, and to the generations to come.

The imaginary power of the uncompleted

Made famous by the Pietà in Saint Peter's, Rome, Michelangelo was commissioned to execute sculptures for the tomb of Pope Julius II. The project was never realized and the statues of the "prisoners" remained unfinished. As they are, they incarnate the artist's contemplation of the struggle of mind over matter. The prisoner, restrained by a fragile bond, overcomes his condition through sleep: a dreamer is free. Offered by Michelangelo to the Florentine exile Roberto Strozzi, the two "Slaves" were given to the king of France. They entered the Louvre in 1794.

See photo p. 52

Man and his finest conquest

Horse of Marly (marble), Coustou, 1739-1745. Height: 3.55 m.

At the end of his reign, Louis XIV developed a passion for the park of the Château de Marly and its decorative features: waterfalls, ponds, groves, and also marble statues. They were dispersed under the Regency in 1719. In 1739, Louis XV decided to commission some large-scale statues from Guillaume Coustou for the château's horse-pond. The Administration of the King's Buildings chose the theme of wild horses neighing and rearing, restrained by men whose faces or hair styles represent the different continents.

A homage to human energy, this scene of a training session, taken from a live model, produces an instantaneous effect. The painter David had this statue and its counterpart placed at the entrance of the Champs Élysées in 1795. They both found refuge in the Louvre in 1984, and exact replicas were set up in their place.

Clay, a child and gentleness

Louise Brongniart aged five, Houdon, 1777

I n the vast domain of sculpture, portraiture has a place apart. It is a genre that has always fascinated models as much as artists. This fascination reflects human beings' desire to preserve a better likeness of their face than in a drawing or a painting: a three-dimensional one. Even the pharaohs wanted to make eternal the one thing they had that was truly unique: their head. For the artist it is a tremendous challenge that goes well beyond the simple idea of pleasing or displeasing. Over and beyond the precision of line and volume, the deep inner truth of the person has to be found, its real duration conveyed in the expression of a mere instant. In modelling the bust of the daughter of the architect Brongniart, Houdon — as in other portraits of people close to him — has been able to express the charming ambiguity of childhood that lies between seriousness and the spontaneity of innocence.

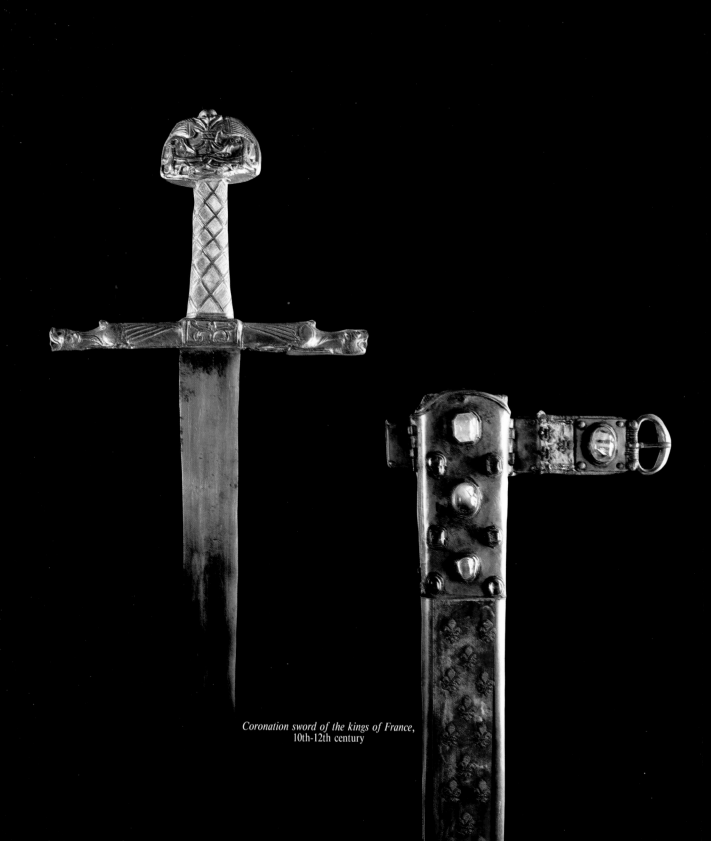

Coronation sword of the kings of France,
10th-12th century

Objets d'art

This was one of the very first collections, figuring in the Convention's decree of 27 July 1793 which founded the museum. In the same year part of the treasure of the Abbey of Saint Denis also entered the Louvre: objects associated with the coronation of the kings of France and precious vases set at the request of Abbot Suger. Three years later it was the turn of Renaissance bronzes and precious stones from the royal collections, followed since by an uninterrupted succession of acquisitions and donations. This section, which presents objects that set the stage for life in bygone centuries, has the irresistible charm of infinite variety.

Golden fish in green water

Serpentine paten (stone), first century B.C. or A.D., 9th century setting. Diametre: 17 cm.

A paten is a bowl made of precious metal in which the priest places the host during a celebration of mass. This masterpiece was created by two artists working quite independently of one another and separated by nine centuries. In the centre lies the bowl, made from a green stone called serpentine, incrusted with golden fish, and dating from Roman antiquity — from the first century either B.C. or A.D. The gold setting uses cloisonné technique: the goldsmith contructed little recesses containing enamel or coloured glass paste. At regular intervals it is decorated with pearls and precious stones. The alliance of these two objects has given birth to a genuine creation. The mounting fully respects the ancient object, and the result speaks for itself. For the early Christians, the fish signified Christ and the apostles were fishermen. This paten accompanied a chalice given to the Abbey of Saint Denis by Charles the Bald.

"The King is dead, long live the King"

The Louvre is the depository of the most ancient treasures in the land, such as this coronation sword of the kings of France. The objects used in the coronation ceremony were kept with the 'treasure' of the Abbey of Saint Denis, to the north of Paris. The blade is of steel, the handle, pommel and guard are in gold, decorated with beads of glass or lapis lazuli.

Tradition has it that this was Charlemagne's sword, christened 'Joyful'. Naturally, all its recipients fervently wanted to embellish it. The pommel and the plate with a plant motif on the guard can be dated to the tenth and eleventh centuries, while the dragons on the two arms of the "cross" (with pearls for eyes) belong to the late twelfth century. The handle with fleur-de-lis decoration dates from the thirteenth century.

This weapon, and the spurs also conserved in the Louvre, are the most ancient royal emblems of France whose whereabouts are still known.

See photo p. 58

A passionate artist and chemist

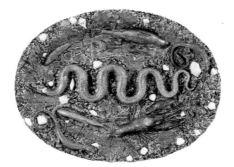

Decorated basin, in relief (varnished earthenware), Bernard Palissy, c.1560

What a strange man, this Bernard Palissy! He was fascinated by ceramics, wanting at all costs to penetrate the secret of enamel. At a certain temperature, metal-oxide powders are transformed into a paste which, when cooled down, shines likes coloured glass, but is much stronger. This is enamel, a material that, like the humble pottery on which it is laid, can last for centuries.

The famous tale is worth retelling, for it is exemplary. One day Palissy realized that he had to stoke the fire in his oven, but he did not have enough wood. Nothing else mattered to him, so he smashed up his furniture and threw it into the furnace. Suddenly, the enamel was there; he had succeeded! Success went to the stubborn child who wanted to complete the task on is own. Yet in the choice of subject matter, we see the creative, innovative man. Following the advice of that universal genius Rabelais, he set himself to observing snakes, fish and lizards in their natural environment and he teaches us in turn to look, and come to know.

A treasure of pure carbon

The Regent

Diamonds never deteriorate. They cross centuries with impunity. The successive sovereigns who have enriched their collections with this one did not perhaps realize that it was the diamond, the so-called ''Regent'', which was in fact keeping count of its owners. The story begins in 1698 with its discovery in India. Thomas Pitt, the governor of Madras, acquired it in 1702. It was brought to England to be handed over to the finest diamond cutters,who succeeded in cutting it to perfection. The Regent (hence its name) purchased it in 1717 for the crown of France. The diamond adorned the coronation crowns of Louis XV and Louis XVI. From then on it would be part of the image of French sovereigns, appearing in 1801 on the guard of the First Consul's sword and then on Napoleon's broadsword in 1812. After glistening at Charles X's coronation and on the diadem of Napoleon III's wife, it entered the Louvre as a work of art, a national treasure and a witness to France's history.

A table that was ahead of its time

Just as it is difficult for us to imagine the time when cathedrals were white, not to mention the period when Greek temples were painted in bright colours, so we have to make a real effort to imagine what our ancestors thought about the furniture of their day. When, in 1784, Dominique Daguerre, haberdasher in the rue Saint Honoré, delivered this writing-desk signed by the master cabinet maker Weisweiler to the royal furniture repository, it provoked the astonished admiration of Marie-Antoinette. Nothing like it had ever been seen before. The sides of the table are of steel, the feet of bronze. The tabletop is lacquered and has a central panel forming a writing stand.
Even functionality has not been overlooked: a small, very handy waste-paper basket is fixed to the base.

Editorial Direction
Daniel Sassier

Book design Rampazzo & Ass.

Picture research
Françoise Faucheux

Photographic credits
Réunion des Musées Nationaux, Paris.
Except:
Page 43: G. Dagli-Orti

Law of july 16, 1949
on children's books

N° d'éditeur 10025608
Imprimé en Espagne par Fournier A. Gráficas, S.A.-Vitoria
ISBN 2.09.240403-2